My father was a landlord and an educated person, my mother was an educator throughout her life. She met with a car accident and died, it was sudden and extremely shocking. I still remember when she left her clothes were hung on a closet hook, her janamaz (prayer mat) place where she used to pray, how a person leaves the world, no time is fixed. She got out of this world leaving us all behind on our own. I did remember, for 5 days, tears were rolling down my cheeks and I can't express the how I was feeling. This was different, how your loved ones leave you behind, who you had no idea of even not seeing for a few minutes. The whole family was upset,

then we adapted to the new circumstances. We were sad and dejected. We were very privileged of having every facility in our life. My father would take care of us more than ever before. But you cannot fill a gap of a mother. Mother is a name of sacrifice, love and standing there to help if any situation arises.

My mother's last words were, "O God, I'm your creature, please help me, I do not want to lead a life depending on others, please help let me die".

She had many bones in her body broken. May her soul rest in peace. She was very pious lady and would fast on every Friday and helped needy people.

IMAGINATION

Lying in the bed imagining the fairy tales-like dreams story, happiness everywhere, luxuriousness and these fantasies continued every night and everyday was like a factory of dream. The day I graduated, the most of the aunties who'd always visit our home, would stare at me and tell my mom, "she is beautiful". I was 3rd in the home, excellent in my studies, and my hobby was to lie in the bad and to dream for hours about my future and marriage, I was engaged with my cousin from the beginning, means when I was 6 years old. Everyone in my family would say, she would fly to Belgium, my cousin's family was living in Brussels. A city popular for diamonds and my fantasy was like there would be diamonds. Once I made my marriage card, it was a fantasy card, I colored it like I spread my whole dream on it, I have never had any affiliation with Imran (my cousin) or his family. Many families would come for me and were rejected and just told that she was already engaged, I didn't had any idea, maybe he had some health issues and our engagement was finished, it was a big shock for me, my dreams were shattered. I was a little upset but because in reality I had no affiliation so it was not really that much shocking to me. You can come out of anything if you had no emotional affiliation, any relation only hurts, if you take it too deeply, it's you who decide, how you're going to take the situation, whether serious or light. I just moved on and waved another dream and flung around it, lying in bed, chasing a fantasy like life and dreaming that I would love my partner very much.

Just after a month, on a sunny day, I was wearing a green half sleeves dress and my mother's golden bangles. Aftab's (my husband) mother and a woman who too knew my father's family came in our house. Aftab drove the car and stood out while the woman came in. My brother took him to drawing room. Aftab's mother asked my family to make me her daughter-in-law. My father said that he would take some time to contemplate. I could not see Aftab because in our family it was not allowed to even meet or see. My younger sister could have managed to see him so I asked her and she told me that she could only see his ear and that, his ears were beautiful. This took me 2 and a half months and it was my barat (wedding ceremony), having bundles of dreams in my eyes about my ideal husband. I would always think that he would like this and he'd be like that. He was jolly nice person. We went to Murree, enjoyed very much and a fairy-tale-like story was projecting.

I was a happy relax type of girl, I would become happy when I wore new dress. My life was circulating around like very common things and my communication was not very good.

I was trained to get into any mold according to changing circumstances. So I was happy. My mother-in-law was a kind lady, she wouldn't let me do any work and even cooked meals for me. Also they had a maid, she'd do all the house sweeping, doing the dishes and washing the clothes, so I was enjoying all the time. Our evenings were in hotels mostly dining out. Once I remember, my husband took me to POF Hotel, I never had taste buds for soup before. He asked me that do you want to have some soup and I said "Yes". I poured a little soup and then mixed 2 spoons of each of three sauces because I didn't know how much to put, which ruined the soup. When I took first spoon of it, it was coming back like a vomit situation and my husband asked, "How's the soup?" and I like Mr. Bean, hiding the emotions, replied by smiling, "Yes, it's very tasty". It was a very awkward situation, I was trying to finish the soup but still left half the bowl of soup.

My life was circulating around clothes, lipsticks, shoes and jewelry. I most of the time didn't put on any makeup because I didn't know how to apply the makeup properly. My brother-in-law's wife was a makeup expert! One day my husband took me to a parlor for learning makeup techniques. I was admitted as a trainer and I did a two-week course for learning on how to apply makeup. This was interesting. I've always had an urge for studying, I did a poultry farming course for six months since my husband was a poultry-businessman and I was also wanting to accompany him. He allowed me to do the course. He was a broad minded person but very short tempered.

He helped me self-develop my talents, I learnt how to bake or make a pizza because I was mostly interested in learning, maybe, to become educator was in my DNA.

I was a philosopher in myself. Because my major was in philosophy, so I could judge people very keenly.

I got know that how different the people from different classes would behave, how diversity is the beauty of our world. There's no one perfect or imperfect but there are people with different talents, different natures and different hobbies. But they are all same in feelings, when you treat them good they feel good, when you treat them bad, they feel sad.

Their languages might be different but there body language is always readable. You can judge a happy soul or a dejected soul.

In the beginning whenever I had a fight with my husband, I'd avenge myself and fight would become worse because I believed that my points are valid, I always thought that I was right and I was never ready to surrender. But it was me who always said sorry to my husband whether it was my mistake or his mistake, this became my habit to say sorry and his habit to start a fight. But this is a part of life, but he was a loving partner so was I. Whenever there was a marriage in our family, it was always the center of my whole world that I must look most beautiful, I'd plan to wear dress matching, jewelry, hair style, shoes and so on. I was a carefree person and didn't know that life has more meanings and different shades. I was leading a life when I was worried about very trivial matters of life which were of no importance but because I was not transformed.

Transformation occurs only when someone realizes that in the consequences of realizing the finality of life, an inability to mourn or impact of the confrontation on the super ego. This was a life which has no aim, no goal, just passing the time, I've had not discovered myself I was in a shell, fearful, fearful of everything. Apparently everything was fine but in reality, I was not myself, I was living for people, people were always on my mind. I set all my standards according to the others. I had no distinct point of my own views. I didn't know the importance of mentoring. Since then I didn't had any mentor in my life. I had no critical point of views from myself, and if, in reality; you cannot think critically you cannot not have your higher self! The reality was I didn't accept myself yet. So time was passing. I used to think that eating three times a day was a work but not it was a luxury, when you are comfortable when you have free time for yourself. I couldn't connect with others. When you are spiritually weak you find a 'dot' like it's the worlds, but when you are spiritually strong then you find the universe like a 'dot'! So, spirituality counts very much. Physical beauty has a self-life but spirituality is eternal, it even keeps you alive when you are physically dead. I would talk but not from heart, I wasn't deep. I was busy that I was just lost in talk. I have no meditation, I had no idea that inside every person is a universe. Even a beggar, a garbage man has a soul which needs to be cherished. My world was revolving around me, I didn't know that I would not discover the universe unless I come out of myself, my ego. I didn't know what manipulation is and how to control myself, my habits.

I was good from heart. After marriage life was becoming practical. A few things changed, now my husband's family were my family members and I would go to my father's home like a guest. It was difficult, I would stay there for a week or two and my husband would pick me back. Then came the days when I would stay there for 3 days, even less than 3 days. The life was changing. We always think that life is going to remain like this but go to another point and this life takes twist, on every step of the way life presents different shades, different scenarios, best it changes sometimes, so subtly that we didn't know that it's changing. Sometimes, we are trapped in illusions, so much that we lose the hold of the realities of life. My imagination was strong from beginning. I would love to dream when I couldn't get, I always go through my dreams. I was looking for the opportunities but not creating them. I was looking for easy solution. When you don't believe yourself, no one believes you!

EARLY YEARS

It was on **28TH September 2000**, when I got my son in my lap for the first time. It was one month earlier than expected date. He didn't cry when born and had pneumonia; he was shifted to another hospital located in Islamabad because there wasn't any facility of incubator available there. He remained on the hospital and probably, the incubator for almost 1 month, than discharged, we got him back home. I was a fashion loving person, just dream loving, living in imagination; always wanting to have a perfect fairytale-like life! My husband was cooperative person.

When my son was 6 months old, I noticed there was something which he was missing. Because this was my first experience of having a baby so I couldn't have any idea that what is the age appropriate for doing certain things. So, sometimes I would become very upset when he wouldn't do the things which other children of his age would do. One of our relatives once came in our home, she called my son and there was no response; we already had the concern about my son but no one was believing my concerns. Once I fought with my husband that we will take our son to the doctor (audiologist) for checkup. He did the **BARA** test and that was the day which I could still remember as a horrible day of my life; as of sky had fallen on me, my son had terrible hearing loss and doctor told me he would never be able to speak. In his right here there was a hearing loss of

110 DB and on left ear 90-110 DB. I was just a young, having dreams for future, but life takes twists, never go straight, than I understood you need to be very strong that you could adapt yourself according to the different circumstances. Tears rolling down my cheeks as I was sitting on front seat of car having my son in my lap just quiet having an idea of quiet world with no voice. There was sounds of motorcycles and cars people around me but I was unable comprehend anything, I was like quiet in a quiet word listening but feeling there is no sound around me very colorless world. Our world has the beauty of sound; if all the sounds are extracted out of this world, the quietness would

eat us away. The first feeling which came to my mind was how he will tell me how he feels, how he will share the things with me I was thinking of picture when I was holding his hands, on the other side was his father holding his hand, both had a connection of hands but not of sound. For a week, I was into imaginations and visualizing that how would I accomplish it all. It needed a number of steps, first was to get him best quality hearing aids with less noise. So, first we got his behind-the-ear hearing aid with the front receiver which was attached to his chest. Because the loss was severe, the main hurdle was, he was unable to hear in the first place. So, I got him a lot of toys with different sounds to let him interact with all sounds as much as possible. I made him do muscle exercises like blowing the candle and filling the balloon. I would often give him massage on daily basis. I transformed my life into just putting my efforts into him. My focus was just my son's speech. He was sensitive to cold, would have constipation for most of the time. My dream of luxury life was lost somewhere. I bought hearing aids which were digitalized and a lot more improved than the previous one. Listening was still the biggest challenge with those hearing aids, because he was almost nearly two years old. I was struggling intensely, first to buy him quality hearing aids, which could not only amplify sound but also filter the noise. Exercises were still continued, speech therapy was must so, I took courses for speech therapy but believe me practical things are different. I still remember when I would sleep at night, I would always hold my lips close to his ears, reciting all the night prayers, he would feel the vibrations of sound and would recognize difference. Maybe it was fun for him but it was not fun for me. I would become tense when I would not pick. His first sounds without the aids were *'Ba Ba Ba'*. It took me 5 hours when he picked water in Urdu as *'Paani'*, he kept saying *'tai'* when finally after 5 hours, he said it correctly as *'Paani'*, I became happy so much that I still can't express. During those five hours we both were sitting near a tub of water, I was dipping his hand in water and making him feel water while saying and repeating the word *'Paani'* again and again. Once he was annoyed he threw his hearing aids somewhere, I kept searching everywhere asked him again and again, "*Where have you thrown the hearing aids*", he took me to a bucket full of water and pointed towards the bucket without uttering any word, I was devastated and helpless but I was not wanting to waste any time, I took them out dried them off, took batteries out, I was drying them with hair drier and as I was angry I slapped him for doing this non sensible thing but after all the efforts, they were out of order. In next few days I planned to buy new pairs of hearing aids but this time cheap one. After 6 months, he had at least 100 words but was unable to articulate them perfectly but I was hopeful now, more than ever before. He was 2 and half years old. I took him to nearby pre-academy which had almost 35 children for pre-education. He cried for a whole week but I was persistent, I was wanting to keep him advance than the children of his age. One of my neighbors, whose son was also enrolled there, said, *"Why are you so cruel to him?"* but I said that social interaction is must for him for solving his problems. In those days luckily we were living in a joint family, I requested all my family members to communicate with him by talking speaking and not by any sort of *'sign-language*. Because I knew, when he will not be given any choice or substitute, he would obviously speak to accomplish his needs. So one thing which strictly followed was not to use any sort of *'sign-language'*. During the times when his hearing aids were out of order, I would took him in my hands while doing all the work and speaking in his ears, I am opening the door of the fridge while opening, emphasizing the word *'opening'* then telling him, "I am taking out an egg, now I will boil this for you", I would also give him egg in his hands to feel the egg, he would show his surprise and then would speak *'eaa'*, not complete word. I would say him in the ear to turn the lights ON while putting his finger and pressing the button then I would say turn the lights OFF, these were whole lot of things which were done practically by holding him close to me, so that I would put my lips near his ears that he could even feel my lips, I noticed that when I let him feel the vibrations created by sound, he would pick the sound soon. Now at the age of 3, he was able to recognize all the letters (A-Z), numbers (1-20), but his speech was still impaired. I took him to speech therapist for one week for professional assistance but then got the idea that the continuous effort was the key to success. At the age of 4 he was in nursery class reading rat, cat and could read three letters words and spellings of ONE, TWO, THREE. I would give him all the vegetables one by one and would repeat the names. I remember once, one of our relatives made fun of me telling me that my son will cook vegetables and why are, but I had a plan to follow. I was formed, I couldn't have left him on his own, and so I did the same recipe with the fruits and all the other things. I realized that how feeling things with hands was so helpful in developing language. I remember how I told him, what 'air' is, I would wave a paper on his face, he could feel the air on his face and would say *'air'*. Once, I almost burnt his finger to tell him about *'hot'* and once put his finger on ice until he said *'cold'* so feeling things was an important aspect of language learning. His language was developing, his brain was developing and he was very intelligent. His intelligence was more than average of other children of his age, as he was more curious at his age, always observing everything. Once I remember that our servant was washing cloths and a pedestal fan was turned ON and as he was curious enough to see how it was moving and what happens when some intervention is done, so he directly put his index finger into the fan and that was when the rotor cut opened the finger's skin and he started screaming and crying, he would touch and handle many things to see how they work and why. To remove his articulation mistakes, I would let him stand on my dressing table facing the mirror and would stand behind him, when he was also able to judge me. I would say cat by speaking, giving vibrations by my lips on his neck, than showing him which parts of tongue I am using. It was not all speaking loud but speaking each word with a gap to make each sound clear. This was really tedious work but now as result was good, so my hope was growing day by day. By every passing day, he was learning something new. When he would speak something new, I would buy him something new of his choice. Now he was 6 years old, studying in 1st grade and could read three word sentences. For instance, *"This is a cat"*, *"That is a dog"*. I would tell him by putting his finger on a thing placed vey near *'this'* and pointing at a distant object, *'that'*. I would give him conceptual lessons, educating him all the time. This required me a lot of patience but I was persistent because I loved my son and love is the no one factor in attaining something bigger or smaller. If you don't have passion, if you don't have love, you will be surely distracted, you will lose your focus and once you lose it, you wouldn't be able to concentrate, you have to take all those steps which are crucial part of your project. You can reach something by taking little steps. You can reach something by taking little steps. For instance, to have speech, first; letters are important, if letters don't develop, words can't develop, and if words can't develop, sentences can't develop and without sentences, one can't build a story. At age 7, he was able to write 4-lines stories and essays, his speech was little clear. I continued to make him learn 4-line stories and essays, on *"A Table"*, *"A Chair"*, *"A Cat"*, *"My School"*, *"My Best friend"*. I remember when I told him about his friend, how I told him his physical friend's physical features, so I got to know that children always learn practically.

One of my conclusion at this point was, all human behaviors are learned behaviors. Language learning is not only crucial to express yourself but it helps you to think critically and judge and identify different behaviors. At this age, I always kept him with me whether I was at a funeral or at a marriage ceremony, telling him the story of dead person or a groom. I made it my habit to generate stories of my own to just explain him well, what is being going on in his environment. Now he started asking questions, and on the other hand, I started using two languages, one was *Urdu* and the other was *English*. On every question, I would give him a lecture, then I realized that lecturing is a good tool, we must explain the things well to our children. We should give them a whole lot of information, which they can use to interpret differences. Once I and my husband had a small argument-fight, my son at once judged at once and asked me what happened, he became sharp to analyze emotions.

I would deliberately let him to have a dialogue with different people so he could listen different voices tones and pitches and analyze the difference. Now his practice was about judging different voices and recognizing them even when they were speaking from behind. So, in our classes we should provide our children with different teachers with different tones, so that children could have the experience of interacting with different persons. Now when he was 7 years old he was becoming emotionally immature, because experimenting different things became his routine. Once he put the juicer (blender) on the stove and turned the stove on, when the blender caught fire and started burning, he; in order to put out the fire, started pouring the water on it, my lovely blender was burnt (while I was writing this, I was smiling and laughing!), once he burnt his nose by lighting the candle with match stick and then putting the lit matchstick back into matchbox close to his face, which resulted in all the matchsticks immediately firing up and burnt his nose, once I was stitching the clothes on manual sewing machine, he sat beside me to see and was curious that how the machine worked, to answer his curiousness he put his hand directly into the moving needle which got stuck in his pinky finger. His experiments were still continued, now he was 11 years old, my 12 hours job was cut into 6 hours and I could've got some time for me. I always loved to be in tip top condition. When he was in 5th grade, I opened my own school. Now he was overcoming barriers and was able to communicate better than before, but there was still a lot to be done. I noticed that he have a good judgement of body language, he was even able to feel the slightest emotions springing out of any person. Once I was in room when he came to me asked me, *"What happened?"* this was a happy surprise to me, this was a dream which came true. I wanted that he could share his feelings with me and now he was ready to listen to me. I than got an idea that listening gives you satisfaction, when someone listens to you compassionately and you know that he/she is giving you his undivided attention. I was sharing, how I was feeling, when I shared my sentences, I realized that sharing emotions is an integral part of learning. I started sharing sensational stories with my son, sometimes giving insight to my own life, my past stories, sometimes just fake stories but stories have more profound affect than mere talk. This was love of a mother, love has different shades, different colors, love is the most beautiful and precious gift a person can give to another person, here I will quote a line which inspired me when I was in 10th grade and was stuck with my brain since then:

"Do not wound the loving hearts, because

loving hearts are like flowers

that can never bloom again and love others for no

reward because *love* itself is a great reward"

Love is really a great reward, I love all the children around the world, I know we are blessed, we are privileged and we must give back something to the humanity, another name for *love* is "*kindness*". I know the meaning of *Love*, I started loving every child as if he has something to share, something to say, he wants our attention, he wants that we should talk to him on his level, I noticed one point:

"All Human beings are in need of attention, they

want Love, they want to be treated with kindness"

So important lesson was to teach them (all children), "how to be caring, how to feel the emotions of others".

We are only creatures on earth who are in-triggered through emotions. Hypnosis is a great tool.

We should use hypnosis technique in our teaching methodology, this is the softest & a pure method. As voice is vibrated, you can feel the vibrations the same way you can feel the vibrations emitted by the love so the highest source of energy is LOVE. You can touch someone's heart with LOVE, when *love* is mixed with your professions, it becomes the divine tool, you can accomplish the miracles with only this energy people say, there a few things which are impossible to do but LOVE has power, Love is LIFE, Love can create new things, Love in itself is a creation, Love is a revival, another name for Love is Humanity another name for Love is kindness, Love is greatest facts, a reality. Love create intuitions Love creates imagination, Imagination has wings, it gets you anywhere even out of this universe. When you Love someone, you feel highest energy and when you have highest energy, you can get through obstacles, because LOVE doesn't knows barriers, it can cut pass mountain, Love knows no distance, it just improves your focus, it just lessens your distractions, it is powerful to have LOVE. People gravitate towards Loving people, Love creates courtesy. Being kind loving and feeling empathy for others are virtuous acts, we should have even those feelings for animals and plants. Such emotions are rewarded by ALLAH (SWT) and rewarded accordingly. This is central to building a solid and powerful self, kindness is a very important attribute. We must do our best, to be kind to all for sake of the ALLAH Almighty and for the sake of goodness. Let us see what the Holy Quran says:

حُبِّهِ عَلَىٰ الطَّعَامَ وَيُطْعِمُونَ
وَأَسِيرًا وَيَتِيمًا مِسْكِينًا

"And they feed the food in spite of love (for) it, (to the) needy, and (the) orphan and (the) captive" (76:7)

قَوْلٌ مَّعْرُوفٌ وَمَغْفِرَةٌ خَيْرٌ مِّن
صَدَقَةٍ يَتْبَعُهَا أَذًى وَاللَّهُ غَنِيٌّ
حَلِيمٌ

"Kind speech and forgiveness are better than charity followed by injury. And Allah is free of need and Forbearing" (02:263)

"The merciful are shown mercy by the All-Merciful. Show mercy to those on earth, and He Who is in heaven will show mercy unto you"
(As-Suyuti)

"To spend of your substance, out of love for Him, for your kin, for orphans, for the needy, for the wayfarer, for those who ask, and for the ransom of slaves"

Love is a heavenly thing, if you cultivate it, you will reap the fruit

Love with you only told you can duchess hole through, you can accomplish unachievable things, projects and goals. When you breathe love in and out, you become divine, you become intuitive and when you have intuition you can see invisible things.

I should write a separate book on love, kindness and empathy. Show with love can kindness sometimes, I was very strict with him but it was all out of love so you was improving. Now his fluency was improving. In 2015 he was in 10th grade computer was his favorite subject. I always prays for Tech Giants-Owners like Bill Gates and Mark Zuckerberg for giving and bringing innovations tech like computers and internet to this world, which is a great source to all who have been through any problem because sometimes, you don't have someone around to socialize them, it entertains you, and it aligns you with the light minded people. Because human beings are social animals, they cannot live without company, without society and another point human beings have hunger for information, and internet quenches this hunger. My husband Malik Aftab's friend, Rafaqat had an accident back in 2003, his backbone was broken, he's still on bed since then, he has been lucky enough to be born in this era of internet and he's socializing through the internet, so I thanks Bill gates, and other Tech-Giant-Owners who've made it possible for everyone to socialize and interact with people. This technology can only be used if someone has good language acquisition.

If this technology is used effectively in the classrooms, this can give wonderful results, this technology has helped my son a lot and this communication gap which he could've faced was covered by the internet. Now he was skillful in computer skills when he passed his matric. I did remember we were so happy. By the time he entered into college, his communication skills were quite improved, he was successfully speaking Punjabi, Urdu and English. In 2018, he was on his way of doing Business Administration (BBA), extremely intelligent, sharing his ideas, a real business minded person. Once I told him that I want to write a book on you, he was reluctant but then I made him realize, that there are many people who go through these issues, and need our help and this book might just help them so he agreed, life is beautiful. Sometimes, when you're going through easy times, you couldn't realize that how comfortable lifestyle you have, you only get to know it when hard time strikes you and then you feel the pain. Pain tells you what 'comfort' feels like, Hurdles tells you what relaxation feels like and you need to pay a hard prize for accomplishing something. Children are duty of our world, they need our utmost attention, they need our company, they need our sympathy and out help and love. Burning desires is number one factor in determining our success, it comes with hardships, gives fruit; very sweet. First imagining

and dreaming the taste of success is
necessary.

TEACHING

If we want to see our children
successful just teach them how to
love humanity, how to be kind and
sympathetic how to persevere, how
to be resilient, how to be passionate,
how to be focused and how to get
away from distractions.
The biggest satisfaction in life is when
you start thinking about others when
you become enough sensitive that
you can feel the pain of others, when

you can spread happiness on others faces and inconsiderate person is of no use, unless and until, he is emotionally connected to others. Love is the biggest energy in the world, when it gravitates it connects you with the universe, it springs out from the hearts, it enhances you spiritual life, you spirits tour soul. Food is for your body, Love is for your soul, you become different by having different mindset, nothing is impossible in the world and we just need to see in different directions.

FIRST PRINCIPLE THINKING

Sometimes you face hardships, these hard times teach you lessons. My son could've become able to speak these languages very effectively because I was not willing to accept the doctor's words. I was just hopeful, being hopeful is a beautiful thing when you face hard times, when you see limitations because hope is generated through imaginations and imagination can even help you reach for the sky. Yet today, when hard times hit me I always put myself on the trajectory of hope, hope keeps me calm and quite. It means that when, One don't mourns, one keeps doors and windows opened to one's inner self and one can walk like, one has left everything in Allah's hands, just hoping for the best.

If you have hope you need another thing which is preparation because success is all about preparation. Prepare yourself in advance for getting desired success, only dreams can't do anything. Pragmatic attitude can bring benefits, when I was struggling with my son, there were many times when I was dejected, I was upset but I never quit on him, I never slowed down, I always tried more, I always worked more, I sweat a lot but never gave up, I continued my efforts so whatever is your goal, just persevere, perseverance is the key, continuity is the key, burning desire is the key. I had a burning desire, my son must speak, now he's speaking three languages behind this whole thing was first a burning desire that he should share his feelings with me, then I never stopped my efforts, whatever the circumstances were. I persevered, I put my child one step ahead of the other children of his age, when on every passing day, he would learn new things, I would become happy, it means you must enjoy every step of the way, sometimes our challenges make us achieve our full potential, we should keep our schedules properly planned in place, I do remember sometimes I emotionally blackmailed him that I'm weeping that he is not trying so emotional strategy has its own worth of all the emotions, Love is the strongest of all, it creates highest energy, if I had given up, I likely wouldn't be where I'm right now. I encourage everyone to reject rejection if someone says no, just say next. I took a leap of faith even when conditions were tough. Everyone needs to pay the price of success, sometimes very heavy price. At first he had a lot of articulation errors in his speech, I didn't see perfection, and I wanted to accomplish the task within the time frame. Embrace being different own it, if u will not own it whoever will own it, your emotional spirits is a precious tool which you can use with your friends because its human nature that they tend to be with somebody who makes them feel happy, somebody who doesn't complicate their life or somebody who hurt them and when we treat others with love it creates high spirit, a lighter soul. A lighter soul travels millions of miles within no time. The power to imagine is a great power which gives you wings to fly, fly to places where you could have never dreamt. You can meet the people, you wish you could've met sometime earlier in your life, you could accomplish the goals which you might could've wished to accomplish. Living a life with purpose is more meaningful and rewarding because you can enjoy every step of the way.

SOUL ETCHING

All etches of body could be forgotten but etching of soul can never be forgotten, it quietens you but awakes your inner self, you get acquainted to a world which you can't explain but just can feel and when feelings occur at so level it gets you close to humanity, when your tears don't roll down the cheeks but are poured on your soul you don't discuss your miseries, don't share your true feelings but you become able to hide them inside you but channelizing is important, when you choose not to answer even when you know to answer but your soul then don't allows you to behave like ordinary people. Soul is the deepest sea, you can't hear the sound of the surface waves, although inside it is a lot of energy, a lot of activity.

FREEDOM

Then comes the time when you feel, you're free, the most precious time, when you feel like in a quite night you are in a boat and that boat is travelling in an opposite direction. When you wave the hand and every second of the way you feel like you are moving apart into world of peace to an unknown world but you are always sure that you are free.

It took me 18 years to burst this bubble, this universe was created on foundation of Love. Heart has a language, I understood that when there was no substitute, I understood the untold story which every person in the world has to share, I understood the feeling springing out of the heart and those precious diamonds couldn't be compared to the physical diamonds. Just try to think, windows and doors which leads to your heart and you know from heart, you can reach the universe. Universe is not outside of your body, it's inside you and you'll find a way. Divine heart is a heart which has Love of God, when I was in 10th grade, I heard this and these lines are still part of me:

"Don't wound the Loving Hearts,
Don't give them endless sorrows
Because
Loving Hearts are like flowers

that can never bloom again"

LOVE AND HUMANITY

Love and humanity are the two sides of the same coins, they can't be ignores, their value can't be undermined. They are very precious gifts, they are roses which a person gifts to another person. A human is a human just because he can take care of others because he can feel the pain of others, if one misses love, nothing is left to be said as human.

UNCONCIOUS AND KINETIC LEARNING

Whatever learning takes place, it takes place unconsciously, your body and your mind is at rest and kinesthetic way of learning where one uses hand and body put him on ease, when body feels relaxed, comfortable and peaceful and at rest, the learning occurs at high speed, so when you deal with children, when you deal with challenges the most important technique is to bring them into a condition where they indirectly learn. They don't know that they are learning. Learning will happen on its own but techniques used are like exercises, body movements and fun way of repeating word's sound because repetition is a process which takes place at a time when a child feels a height of excitement. Different sounds produced from different parts of body are recognized by using their own hands on them. They can sense the vibration on touching those parts even they can feel that how those parts move. They sense the movement, they sense the voice produced from that part, for example, if they are going to learn *'CAT',* you should divide the word cat into 3 sounds, *'KH'* (C), *'A'* (A) and *'T'* (T). First tell them to put their hand on their throat and feel the *'KH'* sound then bring the hand on their lips and feel the word *'A'* then with movement of tongue, tell them how to produce sound *'T'*, while doing *'T'*, you can make them jump up and down, they'll never forget that, how to say *'T'*. This is an unconscious way of learning when children by moving their body parts just feel enjoyment and fun, they'll build coordination and alignment with the teacher and when all feel excitement, learning takes place.

IDEA OF FEATURES

Like every commodity, like every product, like every chemical, human beings have their individual features, individual properties and individual characteristics. As we say that it's a hard material, we can also say that this person is hard, strong, flexible, nice, strength full, neat, disciplined, resilient, persistent and hard working. This person is lazy, abusive, dirty, useless, undisciplined, liar, not persistent, unresilient and unreliable. And the reality is that habits usually don't change, nature doesn't change and people behave the way they are expected to behave. So expectations shouldn't be beyond the properties, one acquires. Expectations must be very realistic, living with different people will become easier when you have idea of these features. The taste from a spoon from a whole pot of rice will be the same, you don't need to check it thoroughly, every bite will have the same taste. The people who fly shallow can't fly high! So you will not get in trouble when you will have the idea of features, you'll not be disappointed, you will not get hurt and you won't be punished. As you can't expect a fish in a desert, you can't expect positive thing from the negative person, you can't expect negativity from a lazy person. Sometimes, as we use the term, "He's reliable", so it has a lot more meaning, try to be reliable. Your fame reaches the people earlier than you do. Sometimes you can write the stories in advance, just keeping the idea of features in your mind, you can't expect infidelity from an infidel person, you can't expect truth from a liar and you can't expect good words from an abusive person. The only words which can move a person from inside, are kind words and words of love. We human beings need attention, we're creatures of love. If you want to deal the relationship, deal it with love, results will be tremendous. The word 'hate' is the bitterest word in the world, all the words which create hatred among the people are bitter words. They make your life like a hell. So be careful, not to choose those words. Try to make a good profile and good features.

LONELINESS IN LEADERSHIP

Sometimes one can feel lonely whenever he steps forward in life. Getting used to loneliness is a necessary step to overcome the grief of loneliness. Sometimes it cuts you off from inside. It tries to kill you, your basic challenge is to overcome the obstacles to move yourself to an upper level. If someone tries to remain in the company of average minded people, he keeps quarreling, he keeps himself busy in fighting with others. So, let yourself know that how you are using your powers, how you are keeping your powers, how effectively you're utilizing you full potential and not just wasting your time and fighting with the people. Overcoming fear is the first step to move forward. Overcome all your fears one by one, fight your enemies

and your distractions quietly.
Understand that just because you're
around others doesn't means that you
can't be lonely, many of us struggle
with loneliness more than ever.
First acknowledging and loneliness
and accept it with full heart is like
deciding to pay bills. Sometimes you
want to get rid of loneliness as its
pain-like condition in the heart which
gives you burns. Someone's loving
remarks can soothe you burns, you
need it, you need love at this stage,
selfless love and love from compatible
person. When you feel like you are in
a lap of flowers.
Acknowledging loneliness gives you
new perspective, you can find growth
in loneliness, it can open the door to
the next idea or change. If we have
the courage to turn towards ourselves

when loneliness hits amazing work can come out from this time.

Taking the time to reflect, write, read and embrace such a time can buy perspective that would never come from the broad rooms. Sometime these moments are so uplifting that it keeps you grounded.

The higher up you go, the more pervasive loneliness becomes. The responsibility of a role that involves making the toughest decisions alone without support, mentor or friend create, creates a sense of loneliness which few of us ever experience. When to get help looking up an old mentor and finding someone who can help you recognize perspective, alignment, priorities and adapt management practices. A man has to

live with the conscience. A man has to live up to his inner feelings.
At last your decisions matter, whatever you decide to take a way matters.

Uniform Education System or Raising Standard of Education

Things have changed in previous three years change which we have never seen in previous 30 years. We need to change our perspective about uniformity in education. The second name should be raising standard of education, not only looking physically at the education but we should use 1st principal thinking that is to dig deeper and to look not only on forms of

Education but from functional perspective. What functions are required out of standard education? That is to prepare them for an unknown yet digitalized World. This digital world could be accessed when one is language-proficient. Text interpretation is the first tool to know the world, we'll be left behind if our children will not be language proficient, and language acquisition is the most important tool any child needs to acquire. As we say this is an era of information technology, all information comes with text interpretation. It has been research that all human behaviors are learned behaviors and brain develops when we learn the language. So we should start overhauling the system by focusing on this crucial step. Taking out some time for just developing their reading skills interpretation of texts through real life example. It is a digital world, we should overhaul our Montessori(s) because kids of today's era are more informed than ever before. Uniform education doesn't mean that high-performing schools should come to one step lower, it means raising standard and reaching out for potential solutions. Numeracy, science skills, social skills, all skills need to be learned through trial and error. One important point here is every child should know how to present his work, how to get out of that comfort zone, how to feel comfortable that no one is scrutinizing him. Our children need to be themselves not someone else. They have their own passions and interests, they have individual weaknesses and as well as strengths, they need to be treated as individuals, they should be given time to just know that we are here to correct mistakes. Mistakes are part of our life. We should just learn from our mistakes. The gratitude and happiness they need to feel everyday not just driven by grades. Our assessments are getting them behind. The kids of this era are wiser because they have exposure to the things which we could never have imagined. In Elite schools children are taken care of, they are loved, so we are needing this standard in our Public Schools but we are having those teachers who come from home with bundle of frustration. We need to discipline our staff to learn how to love our students because our students need individual attention, our appreciation. We need to enlighten our classes with love, respect when we know that our students are not paying lofty fees, when we know that some time our student have not sufficient food to eat , when we know that one of their parents is ill, they don't have enough resources, love has power to make them feel happy. It makes them hopeful that next time would be better time, our children will not walk away from schools, and they will love to come to school. We will get stronger as a nation when no child will be left behind because our future lies in their hands.

Printed in Great Britain
by Amazon

35356236R00043